KRISTI

PURE GOLD

YAMAGUCHI

*Kristi leaps into the air at the end of her routine during the
1992 World Figure Skating Championships.*

K R I S T I
PURE GOLD
YAMAGUCHI

BY JEFF SAVAGE

Taking part BOOKS

DILLON PRESS
New York

Maxwell Macmillan Canada
Toronto

Maxwell Macmillan International
New York Oxford Singapore Sydney

Photo Credits

All photos courtesy of AP—Wide World Photos

Book design by Carol Matsuyama

Library of Congress Cataloging-in-Publication Data

Savage, Jeff, 1961-
    Kristi Yamaguchi: pure gold / by Jeff Savage. — 1st ed.
       p.   cm. — (A Taking part book)
    Includes Index.
    Summary: A biography of the young Japanese-American skater who won the gold medal in women's figure skating at the 1992 Winter Olympics.
    ISBN 0-87518-583-5
       1. Yamaguchi, Kristi—Juvenile literature. 2. Skaters—United States—Biography—Juvenile literature. [1. Yamaguchi, Kristi. 2. Ice skaters. 3. Japanese Americans—Biography.] I. Title. II. Series.
GV850.Y36S28   1993
796.91'092—dc20
[B]   92-42190

Dillon Press
Macmillan Publishing Company
866 Third Avenue
New York, NY 10022

Maxwell Macmillan Canada, Inc.
1200 Eglinton Avenue East
Suite 200
Don Mills, Ontario M3C 3N1

Macmillan Publishing Company is part of the Maxwell Communication Group of Companies.

First edition

Printed in the United States of America

10   9   8   7   6   5   4   3   2   1

CONTENTS

INTRODUCTION

A group of girls wearing ice skates waited excitedly behind a screen as the awards ceremony was about to begin. Out in the middle of the ice rink, the medals podium was being set up. Kristi Yamaguchi stood nervously with the other girls, wondering what she was supposed to do next. She had just won the gold medal in women's figure skating in the 1992 Olympic Games in Albertville, France.

Kristi was a long way from her home in Fremont, California. But her family was in the arena, and she knew all her friends at home were watching on television. She peeked around the screen and saw her mother and father in the crowd and waved at them. They were beaming with pride. So was her coach, Christy Kjarsgaard Ness, who was standing nearby. Kristi giggled.

Overhead, the American flag was unfurled. Kristi looked anxiously at her skating friend, Nancy Kerrigan,

Kristi congratulates teammate Nancy Kerrigan during the medal ceremony at the 1992 Olympic Games.

standing behind her. "Do I have to say anything?" Kristi asked. Nancy didn't know. This was her first Olympics, too.

Then the announcer's voice thundered through the auditorium in French. "*La medaille d'or . . .*" "The gold medal." It was the moment Kristi had been dreaming about since she was a little girl. She couldn't believe it. She was the greatest figure skater in the world—the Olympic champion. She turned around again and looked at Nancy as the crowd roared. Could this really be happening? Nancy laughed and nudged her. "Go on out," Nancy said. "You did it."

Kristi hopped onto the ice and glided out in her black-and-gold costume to the center of the rink, waving to the crowd. She stepped up on the medal podium and smiled as the audience cheered and waved miniature American flags. Kristi was only 5 feet tall and weighed just 93 pounds, but right then she felt as if she was on top of the world.

Midori Ito of Japan, who had won the silver medal, came out and took her place on the stand next to Kristi.

Kristi (center) rides on the shoulders of teammate Rocky Marval during the closing ceremonies of the 1992 Olympic Games.

Nancy was next. She had finished third to win the bronze medal, and as she skated out the crowd roared again. Kristi couldn't stop giggling. She was happy she had won the gold, but she was just as happy for her friend Nancy.

After the ceremony, Kristi was interviewed by a swarm of reporters. She told them, "I dreamed of this since I was a little girl. From the first time I put on skates. But to think that my dream came true. . . ."

Kristi was the first American woman to win the figure skating gold medal since a girl named Dorothy Hamill did it 16 years earlier. When Kristi was six years old and she began skating, she carried a special doll with her everywhere she went—a Dorothy Hamill doll. Now, she thought, there would soon be Kristi Yamaguchi dolls.

STARTING SMALL

K risti Yamaguchi was born on June 12, 1971. A tiny baby, she also had clubfeet, a condition that made her toes point inward. "Her feet were all the way turned in," says her mother, Carole, "and it gave her a lot of problems when she was a baby." To correct her clubfeet, Kristi wore special casts that had to be changed every two weeks. Because the casts were so heavy, sleeping was very uncomfortable, and Kristi often woke up crying.

After a year of wearing the casts, Kristi's feet were straightened. But the doctor advised that she wear corrective shoes for four more years, just to make sure her feet would remain straight. Because she was still a baby, Kristi had to learn to walk while wearing the awkward shoes.

Kristi grew up in Fremont, California, where her family still lives. Kristi's father, Jim, is a dentist, and her mother, Carole, works as a medical secretary. Kristi has a

Watching Kristi practice for her Olympic performance, it's hard to believe she had to learn to walk with her feet in casts.

brother, Brett, who is three years younger, and a sister, Lori, who is two years older.

As a child, Kristi especially liked to play with Lori. When she was four, Kristi went with her mother to Lori's dance class. As Lori danced around the room with the other girls, Kristi looked up at her mother and said, "I want to play, too." Kristi's mother thought it would help Kristi's feet develop if she were more active, so she signed her up in the class the following week. Kristi practiced ballet and tap dance and tumbling, and before long she was very coordinated.

One Saturday morning, Kristi went with her mother to a shopping mall, where an ice skating show was taking place. Kristi had never seen an ice rink before, and she was fascinated by the gleaming ice skates and the pretty costumes worn by the skaters. She wanted to skate, too, but her mother thought the four-year-old might hurt herself if she fell on the ice.

Kristi went home and continued to dream about the ice skating show. Every week or so she would plead with

A group of schoolchildren listen excitedly as Kristi tells them about what it is like to be a skater.

her mother to let her skate. "When you start school, then maybe we'll see," her mother told her.

Kristi entered the first grade and continued to ask her mother to take her skating. "You promised," Kristi said. Remembering her promise, Carole agreed to take Kristi skating. One afternoon Kristi and her next-door neighbor, a boy named Michael Teves, piled into the car and rode with their mothers to the Southland Mall in Hayward, California. It was the same mall where Kristi had first seen the ice skating show.

At the rental booth, a man measured Kristi's feet and brought out a pair of leather shoes with blades on the bottom. "Okay, these are yours," he said. "They should fit you fine." Kristi put on the skates and tried to stand up. Her legs wobbled, her knees buckled, and she tumbled to the floor. Her mother helped her back up and walked her out to the ice rink. Michael followed with the help of his mother, and soon the two of them were standing on the ice.

Kristi's mother held her up as Kristi carefully placed one foot in front of the other on the slippery ice. It was just like learning to walk again. She practiced walking and sliding for an hour and laughed the whole time. When it was time to leave, Kristi's mother went to return the skates. Kristi began crying. "The man," Kristi said,

Kristi whirls around in a dazzling spin.

pouting, "the man said the skates were mine." Kristi's mother explained that the skates would be there next week when they came to skate again.

Kristi returned to the rink the next week, and the week after that. Then she joined the junior skating program and soon learned to stand up on her own. Before long, she was able to glide across the ice and carefully spin in a circle, usually without falling.

She would also go with her mother, every chance she got, to watch the ice skating shows at the Southland Mall. She loved watching the drill team shows and pageants and the big Christmas spectacular. Kristi wanted to skate in these shows, and she knew she had to get better to do so. She begged her parents for private lessons so she could get more instruction from a coach. Seeing how much their daughter loved to skate, they agreed, and Kristi began taking lessons twice a week.

Eventually, Kristi was good enough to enter her first contest. Her mother signed her up for a competition in San Jose with all the six-year-old girls in the area. Kristi wore a pretty pink tutu to the event, and with her parents watching from the stands, she skated as well as she could. She wasn't nervous, and she performed very well.

Afterward, the judges posted the results of the contest on a pole. Her parents scanned the list with the other parents and saw the name at the top of the list: Kristi Yamaguchi. "Oh, my gosh, I think she won," her mother said. "You won, Kristi. You won!" Kristi was the only one who wasn't excited. She looked up at her parents and said, "Oh, that's nice." It didn't matter to Kristi that her name was at the top of the list. She only knew that she had fun skating.

CHAPTER TWO

ON HER WAY

Kristi was seven years old when her mother enrolled her in a summer camp for skaters in Santa Rosa. One of the camp's leaders, a woman named Christy Kjarsgaard, introduced herself to Kristi by saying, "Hi, Kristi. My name is Christy, too." Kristi thought it was very special that she shared the same name with a camp instructor, and Christy Kjarsgaard instantly became her favorite leader.

Christy, likewise, was impressed with Kristi's enthusiasm and talent on the ice, especially for such a small girl. "Kristi was extremely tiny and her jumps were so small," Christy said, "but I remember the determination on her face when she was out on the ice. She really wanted to do each jump properly."

When camp ended and Kristi returned home to Fremont, she told her parents about this instructor

After her performance at the 1992 U.S. Figure Skating Championships, Kristi received a standing ovation.

named Christy. Soon Carole was on the phone with Christy, who was considered a superb skating coach. "Our daughter really likes you and we'd like her to begin taking lessons from you," Kristi's mother said. "Fine," Christy responded, "but only under one condition." The coach explained that Kristi would have to forget everything she had been taught and begin a whole new way of skating. The Yamaguchi family agreed, and serious lessons began.

Four days a week, Mom would wake Kristi at 4:00 A.M. By 4:30, they would be in the car, traveling on a bridge across the San Francisco Bay to a shopping mall in San Mateo. At 5:00 A.M., Kristi would be on the ice, practicing with her new coach. She would skate for five hours. Her mother would wait, either in the car or at a nearby doughnut shop. At 10:00 A.M., Kristi and her mother would return to Fremont and Kristi would hurry to school. After school, Carole would drive Kristi to another skating rink in Dublin. There Kristi would join her other coach, Jim Hulick, to practice pairs skating with her partner, Rudi Galindo.

Kristi discusses her routine with coach Christy Kjarsgaard Ness.

KRISTI YAMAGUCHI: PURE GOLD

"When I look back on it, I worked incredibly hard for a little kid," Kristi said. "I wouldn't get off the ice until I did a particular move right. I kept bugging my mom: Let's go skating."

By the time Kristi was ten, she and her mother were waking up early six days a week. A year earlier, Kristi had attended a national event held in nearby San Jose featuring all the best skaters from the United States. She had come home that night determined to be as good as the skaters she had just seen. She increased the amount of time she spent on the ice.

Five hours of skating in the morning and two hours more in the afternoon left little time for studying and even less for playing with friends. But Kristi loved being on the ice so much that she didn't feel as though she was missing out on anything.

Kristi entered her first serious competition—the California regionals in Stockton—when she was 12. She finished in the top three. This qualified her for the Pacific Coast competition held in Berkeley the following week.

She won the event, qualifying her for the U.S. Nationals to be held in Kansas City the following month.

Kristi flew with her mother to Missouri for the event. The airplane flight was more exciting to her than the event, but she remembers it took a long time to get to Kansas City. In the competition, with 32 girls entered, Kristi took fourth place. She was pleased with her performance, but she had more fun riding up and down the elevators and running through the hallways of the hotel with the other girls.

Kristi was such a talented skater that she was able to compete in the singles events as well as skate with her partner, Rudi, in various pairs competitions. She even competed in the event in Kansas City with Rudi. They had qualified by winning the Pacific Coast pairs event. Kristi and Rudi finished fifth in the U.S. Nationals junior pairs in Kansas City.

The judges were so impressed with Kristi and Rudi that they invited the duo to compete in the world junior championships. The event was being held halfway around the world in the European country of Yugoslavia. And Kristi thought the plane trip to Kansas City was long!

"Kristi was so tired by the time we got to Yugoslavia that when we got on the train she fell right asleep," her mother remembers. "The food was really different, too. But Kristi likes to eat anything, so it didn't matter to her."

Kristi and Rudi represented America well by skating smoothly and finishing fifth overall in the juniors category, which is for boys and girls under the age of 16. To be considered the fifth-best pairs team in the world among the juniors was quite impressive, but Kristi wasn't satisfied. She didn't complain, even to her mother, but she knew inside that she wouldn't be content until she was Number One.

When Kristi returned home, she practiced harder than ever before. This meant that she had even less time to see her friends. Shy by nature, Kristi had a hard time making friends. Often when she was around people her own age, she didn't know how to act. She was so used to behaving like a grown-up when it came to skating that she

Kristi takes a break from skating to attend a hockey game with her friend, pairs skater Natasha Kuchiki.

sometimes forgot that she was barely a teenager.

Because of her skating, Kristi had been attending Centerville Junior High School for only two classes a day and studying with a private tutor in the evenings. But the following year, when she reached the ninth grade, the high school in her area wouldn't let her come to school only part-time. So she had to study at home all the time.

Eventually, a counselor recommended that Kristi find another high school to attend because it was important for her to socialize with other boys and girls. There were five high schools in Fremont, and one of them, Mission San Jose High at the southern end of town, agreed to be flexible with her and allow her to attend school part-time.

Kristi was happier now that she was in school with classmates, and her skating got even better. She worked with Christy Kjarsgaard on her singles skills, polishing her jumps and double jumps, in which she spins around twice in the air before landing. She worked just as hard with Coach Jim Hulick and her partner, Rudi, in pairs competition.

A month after Kristi celebrated her 16th birthday, she qualified for the junior world nationals again—and this time she was determined to win. It wasn't in Yugoslavia

Kristi and her mother take in a tennis game.

this time, but in Brisbane, Australia. She and Rudi took another long airplane flight to the competition, where they competed in pairs and Kristi competed in singles.

In the singles competition the first night, Kristi skated with precision to place second in the compulsory figures. The compulsory figures are a set of very specific moves that each skater has to perform, such as forming a figure 8. This had always been the most difficult portion of the competition for Kristi, and she was pleased with second place.

She finished second again in the short program, which lasts about two minutes and which shows off a skater's jumps and spins. This put her in second place overall, with her favorite portion of the competition, the long program, still to go.

"I knew something changed in her that night," said her coach, Christy. "I saw it on her face—a real determination, a real desire. She grew up that night."

In the long program, which usually lasts about four minutes, Kristi skated beautifully to music from *Madame*

Kristi's graceful style captures the attention of judges and fans every time she goes out on the ice.

Kristi receives a warm welcome from her fans in Texas during a visit.

Butterfly. She landed cleanly on all of her jumps and double jumps, even the difficult double axel. She placed first in the long program, and after the judges tabulated the scores, the overall winner was announced: Kristi Yamaguchi.

The American team was overjoyed. When Kristi came off the ice, she spent the next 20 minutes hugging everyone she knew. She thought back to the time when she had won her first competition and responded, "Oh, that's nice," because it didn't matter. This time, it mattered very much.

But Kristi didn't come all the way to Australia just to win one title. She wanted to win two. The following night, she teamed up with Rudi in the pairs competition. As they began to skate, she inspired him by whispering, "Get going," in his ear. They performed their routine perfectly and won the world junior title.

Suddenly, there was a new young lady on the international skating scene, and her name was Kristi Yamaguchi.

CHAPTER THREE

THE BIG LEAGUES

Everything was happening so quickly for Kristi. She had won several skating competitions in the junior ranks. Suddenly, reporters were calling her house and writing articles about her in the local newspapers. She was getting teased by her friends at school about being a big celebrity. But the funny thing was, Kristi really *was* becoming a celebrity.

Kristi's mother continued to drive her to practice each morning while her father worked in his dentist's office. The Yamaguchis did the best they could to pay for Kristi's lessons—but it was very expensive.

"People complain about the expense of sending a child to college. I liken it to that," Kristi's father, Jim, said. "At some universities, the cost is, what, fifteen or twenty thousand dollars a year? I feel like we've been sending Kristi to Harvard for twelve years. It's probably even more

Kristi warms up before a practice session.

than that." To help save money, Jim drove a ten-year-old sedan instead of a newer car. "There have been many sacrifices, especially financial ones," Kristi's mother, Carole, said.

Kristi's brother and sister were proud of her, but sometimes they felt that she was the favorite child. "There were times when they maybe resented the extreme hours devoted to Kristi," Jim said. "Still, they realized she was giving up a lot to do what she did."

One of the things Kristi never got to do was go out on Friday nights with her high-school friends. She had to be up early on Saturday mornings for practice. Kristi's brother and sister definitely lived more "normal" child-hood lives. And they both had their own interests. Lori was a national baton-twirling champion. Brett, who was ten inches taller than Kristi, was the captain of his high-school basketball team.

Meanwhile, Kristi continued to excel at skating. She had shown that she could compete against girls her own age. But what about the women? Was Kristi good enough to compete against the grown-ups? She didn't know.

In her first big competition against the older girls, Kristi finished tenth at the U.S. Nationals, coming in behind great skaters like Debi Thomas and Jill Trenary. This was early in 1988, and Kristi devoted the entire year to developing a strong style on the ice. She didn't want to just skate and jump and leave it at that. She wanted to project excitement and enthusiasm on the ice. She wanted to leave an impression on the crowd. Kristi decided that 1989 would be her year.

It began with the U.S. Nationals again. Kristi had finished tenth the previous year, and her goal this time was to be in the top five. She would also compete in pairs with Rudi, but by now her singles skating had become a little more important.

Then, several months before the competition in February, her pairs coach, Jim Hulick, revealed to her that he was seriously ill. He had been diagnosed as having colon cancer, and he had to spend six weeks undergoing treatments and removing malignant areas. He was forced to abandon his coaching, letting go of all his students except Kristi and Rudi. They were his star pupils and he just had to keep coaching them, no matter what. As the U.S. Nationals approached, Kristi and Rudi decided that they owed their coach the best performance they could possibly give.

The night of the competition in Baltimore, Maryland, Coach Hulick looked on from the far end of the ice as Kristi and Rudi skated to music from the movie *Romeo and Juliet.* One week earlier, he had undergone a blood transfusion so he could go with them to the competition. Kristi and Rudi got a roar from the crowd as they landed a triple flip. They were the only pair in the world who could do it. Later, they performed side-by-side double axels, and the crowd roared again.

Kristi and Rudi blew away the competition and won the gold medal, something no one ever expected from such a young pair. Coach Hulick was so proud of his students that he was still smiling an hour after the competition ended. When reporters asked Jim about

Kristi and her former pairs partner, Rudi Galindo, stun the audience at the 1989 U.S. Nationals.

KRISTI YAMAGUCHI: PURE GOLD

Kristi, he looked at them and said, with a straight face, "She's superhuman."

But Kristi wasn't finished just yet. She still had the ladies singles competition to worry about. Her goal, she remembered, was to finish in the top five. After the compulsory round she was in eighth place.

But then Kristi took over. She finished second in the short program and, after four hours of sleep, came back in the afternoon to perform her long program. In the seven minutes she was on the ice, Kristi executed seven triple jumps, in which she spins around three times in the air before landing. When she finally came to a stop, she flashed a big smile that brought the audience to their feet. She won the long program and finished second overall. It was such an exciting performance that Kristi got a bigger ovation from the crowd as the silver-medal winner than gold medalist Jill Trenary did.

Afterward, the media swarmed around Kristi. She was so embarrassed that all she could do was giggle. With each question the reporters asked, Kristi stopped to think about an answer and then would say "yes" or "no" and then start giggling again. Kristin Matta, who works for the U.S. Figure Skating Association, watched Kristi laugh through the interview and knew right then she had to teach Kristi how to be interviewed. So, for the next few weeks, Kristi practiced doing interviews and watched tapes of other skaters being interviewed. "She's such a sweet girl and she learned how to project her nice image," Kristin Matta said. "She's very shy, but once she knew how to speak up and not be embarrassed, everyone saw how charming she is."

Back home in Fremont, Rei Yong, the editor of the Mission High school newspaper, did a story about Kristi. She thought he was cute, and for the interview they had to go out to dinner. Later that year, Rei would take Kristi to the Mission High Senior Ball.

Everything was going well for Kristi until her singles coach, Christy Kjarsgaard, decided to move to Canada to get married. Her new name became Christy Kjarsgaard Ness, and Kristi had to begin flying every other week to

Screaming fans swarm around Kristi asking for autographs.

Edmonton, Canada, to practice a few days at a time. She continued to practice at home with Rudi and pairs coach Jim Hulick.

But Kristi was more interested in her singles career. The day after she graduated from Mission High, in June of 1989, she moved to Canada to live with Christy and her husband, Andrew Ness. Her parents were sad to see her go, but they knew it would help her skating. "I'm excited to go up to Canada because I hear there will be a lot of good skaters training up there this summer," Kristi said at the time. She brought only one suitcase of clothes and a pink stuffed pig that was given to her by her best friend, Allison Takamoto.

Rudi did not want to live in Canada, so Kristi returned to Fremont once a month to practice pairs skating for several days with him. But late in 1989, everything changed for the worse. Coach Hulick, who had been suffering from cancer for quite some time, died in December. Then, five days later, Kristi's grandfather died, too. It was a horrible time for her and she wept for days. She tried to concentrate on her skating but it was no use.

The following month, in a big competition in Halifax, Canada, Kristi couldn't focus on her routines. All she could think of was her pairs coach and her grandfather. She missed them both terribly. She finished fourth in the singles and fifth in the pairs. Neither performance was

Once Kristi decided to concentrate on her singles skating, she became an overnight star.

very good by her standards, and she was extremely disappointed.

Although Kristi didn't know it at the time, the poor showing in Halifax was one of the most important moments in her life. She was suddenly overcome with a motivation to succeed like never before. Skating experts suggested that it might be wise for her to choose between singles and pairs, and to concentrate solely on one or the other.

Kristi agreed. She picked singles and dropped pairs. Rudi was crushed. Never again would Kristi Yamaguchi and Rudi Galindo team up to win a medal. Kristi felt terrible about ending their partnership, but it was something she knew she had to do.

Kristi went about training with renewed enthusiasm. She began a weight-lifting program to build up her strength. She did various lifts, such as leg extensions, toe raises, and squats for her legs, and dips, curls, and military presses for her upper body. Four months later, she beat Jill Trenary at the Goodwill Games to win the gold. Later

A triumphant Kristi waves to the crowd after winning the gold medal at the 1992 U.S. Championships.

that year, she beat Midori Ito of Japan at Skate America to win another gold.

"Kristi's bad performance in Halifax was a breakthrough," her coach, Christy, said after Skate America. "Kristi has grown up this year. She is stronger this year physically and she has matured. You are seeing a different performer out there."

When Kristi went home for Christmas at the end of 1990, she was asked to skate in the Brian Boitano and Katarina Witt show at the Cow Palace in San Francisco. Boitano and Witt were Olympic champions, and Kristi was honored just to have been asked. She gave a nice performance and received a loud ovation from the fans. "It was like a dream come true," she said. Skating had always been as much work as anything else for Kristi, but on this night it was all fun. Still, Kristi had more than just fun on her mind. The 1992 Olympics were only a year away, and she had big plans.

CHAPTER FOUR

GOING FOR GOLD

Kristi missed her family. She was a long way from home, living in Canada and practicing almost eight hours a day at the Royal Glenora rink. "I miss seeing my family every day," she said, "but on the other hand, I talk to my mom quite a bit on the phone. It's been all right." Christy Kjarsgaard Ness also talked often with Kristi's mother. She would call her sometimes when Kristi had a bad day and always before approving Kristi's dates or movie outings.

Kristi certainly missed her mother when it came to wearing outfits, because Carole always took in her clothes to fit. Kristi was almost 20 years old, but she weighed just 93 pounds and wore a size 1 in clothes and a size 3 children's shoe. For such a petite woman, Kristi had developed a dynamic presence on the ice, and she found out just where she ranked with the rest of the world in the

Kristi performs a difficult flying camel on her way to winning her second straight World Championship.

last big event before the Olympics—the world championships in Munich, Germany.

The compulsory figures, Kristi's least favorite of the
three programs, had been eliminated from ladies figure
skating competition a few months earlier. This left only
the short and long programs. In the short, Kristi was
superb. She performed several triple jumps, and the
judges ranked her first going into the long program.

But there was one problem. The latest rage in ladies'
figure skating had become the triple axel, where the skater
spins around completely three times in the air before
landing. Despite her strength training, Kristi wasn't quite
able to accomplish such a jump. Two other competitors
could: Tonya Harding of the United States and Midori Ito
of Japan. Even Kristi's mother wasn't sure that Kristi
could win the long free-skate program and the gold. "I
don't know if she's mentally tough enough yet," Carole
said. "And she doesn't have that triple axel."

It turned out she wouldn't need it. Midori Ito hurt
herself in the warm-ups by crashing into another skater,

Tonya Harding (silver medalist), Kristi (gold medalist), and Nancy Kerrigan (bronze medalist) proudly show off their medals at the 1992 World Championships.

and she didn't perform well at all. Tonya Harding landed safely on her triple axel, to the delight of the crowd, but then she stumbled on two other jumps. Kristi, who was last to perform, jumped visibly higher than the other competitors and safely landed six triple jumps.

Kristi was awarded a perfect 6.0 from one judge and

received 5.9s from the rest to win by a landslide. Harding finished second and Nancy Kerrigan third, to give the United States a sweep of the medals. It was the first time one nation had ever finished 1-2-3 in a world competition. Kristi, always quiet and shy, just couldn't contain her excitement. She let out a shriek that pierced through the Olympiahalle for all the fans to hear. "She's such a finished skater," Tonya's coach, Dody Teachman, said. "Coming into this I knew Kristi would be our competition."

All those years of practice finally seemed to be paying off for Kristi. She may not have been able to do a triple axel, but she could do everything else better than anyone else. Still, there were ten months to go before the Olympics. Maybe, Kristi thought, that would be enough time to learn the triple axel.

Kristi practiced it over and over. The months went by and she just couldn't quite get it. One weekend late in the year, her mother came up to Edmonton to watch her practice. There were seven other skaters on the ice, but her mother didn't notice. There was a Japanese television crew trying to schedule a lunch date with Kristi, but her mother didn't notice. Her eyes were riveted on her daughter as she tried to leap in the air, spin, and land softly. Instead, she landed, stumbled, and fell. Watching her daughter try so hard was difficult for Carole. "It is the one thing I cannot give her," she said. "I cannot give her the triple axel."

Finally, in February of 1992, the Olympics arrived. Kristi flew to the little town of Albertville, high in the French Alps, where the Olympic competitors for all the sports were gathering for the opening ceremonies. The skating events wouldn't be held for almost two weeks, but Kristi's parents and coach felt that she would be missing out if she did not attend the opening. "If she misses the opening ceremony and then skates badly," her coach, Christy, said, "what are you left with for your Olympic experience?"

Kristi roomed with Nancy Kerrigan at the Olympic village, and she got to meet a lot of skaters and other

KRISTI YAMAGUCHI: PURE GOLD

athletes during the days leading up to the figure skating competition. Kristi practiced her routines each day in private at a little rink about five miles away. She still couldn't do the triple axel, but she hoped her strength, poise, and vibrant appearance would be enough. Kristi knew that the Olympic women's figure skating champion would become the sports queen of the world. She would get endorsements, contracts, pictures on magazine covers and cereal boxes, and all the attention any one person could stand.

Finally, the moment she had been waiting for came. The short program would be held on Wednesday, and the long program two days later on Friday. U.S. coach Don Laws predicted that Kristi had the best chance of winning, saying, "Kristi has the ideal temperament for a skater. She trusts her coach, her parents, and her program."

On Wednesday night, with thousands of people in the stands at the Olympique Halle de Glace and millions more all over the world watching on television, Kristi prepared herself with the rest of the skaters. Then, right

Kristi tears through her original program during the 1992 Olympic Games in France.

Kristi charms the crowd.

Kristi soars over the ice to take the Olympic gold medal.

before she went onto the ice for her two-and-a-half minute performance, Kristi got a special boost. Dorothy Hamill, who had won the Olympic gold in the same French Alps 16 years earlier, and who had always been Kristi's all-time idol, came up to Kristi and offered her some words of encouragement. "She reminded me how hard I'd worked," Kristi said.

Kristi glowed with excitement. Then she hopped out onto the ice and performed beautifully, completing a breathtaking triple-Lutz, double-toe combination to the

Midori Ito (silver medalist), Kristi (gold medalist), and Nancy Kerrigan (bronze medalist) celebrate their victories at the Olympic Games.

roar of the crowd. Tonya Harding and Midori Ito, the two skaters who could perform the elusive triple axel, both fell. Midori was fourth after the first round. Tonya was sixth. France's Surya Bonaly was third. Kristi's Olympic roommate, Nancy Kerrigan, stood in second place. And Kristi? She was where she knew she could be: in first place. But there was still the long program to go in two days.

On Friday night, with the women attempting more difficult jumps than ever before in history, almost all the competitors fell. All, that is, but Kristi. Midori Ito finished second overall—she fell. Nancy Kerrigan won the bronze—she fell. Tonya Harding was fourth and Surya Bonaly fifth—they fell.

Kristi touched her hand to the ice on a triple-loop jump, but it was a minor mistake and the only one she made in the four-minute program. She finished first in the long program, and, combined with her first-place finish two days earlier in the short program, it was a clear first-place victory. Kristi was the Olympic champion—the greatest skater in the world.

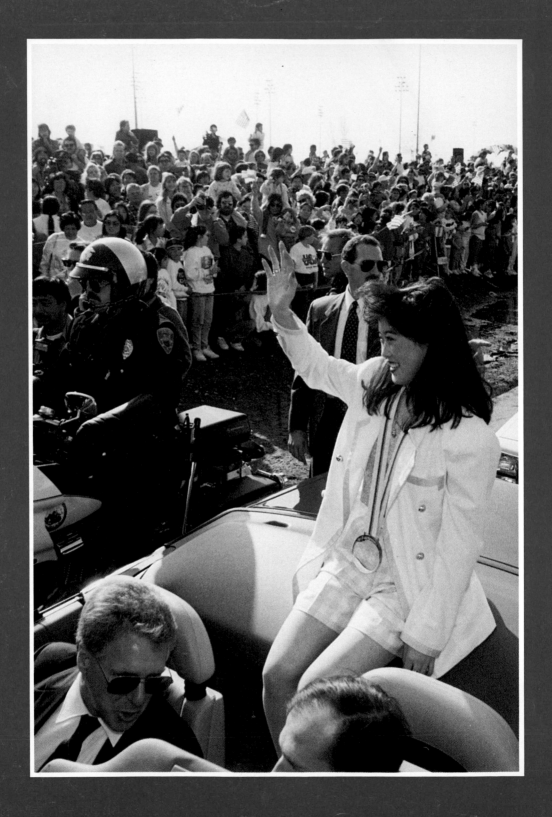

CONCLUSION

On February 21, 1992, all of Kristi's childhood dreams came true. She had become the Olympic figure skating champion and a celebrity all in one night. Afterward, Kristi said, "I suppose things are going to be a little different, even though I feel the same inside. I know something really special just happened."

Her life truly did change the moment she was awarded the gold medal. Within a week, she was on the cover of *Sports Illustrated*, *Newsweek*, several other magazines, and a cereal box. She appeared on the "Arsenio Hall Show," "Good Morning America," and a host of other television programs.

Then she began making commercials. Among the products Kristi has endorsed are Evian water, Kraft foods, 3M products, Kellogg's cereal, California raisins, Durasoft contact lenses, and Ray-Ban sunglasses. She

Kristi's fans welcome her home after her Olympic win.

even endorses a German textiles company and has her own line of designer clothes.

She is a spokesperson for the American Lung Association and Christmas Seals. In December of 1992 she lit the Christmas tree in New York's Rockefeller Center, and in January 1993 she was the Grand Marshal for the Fiesta Bowl Parade in Arizona.

With all the attention surrounding her and the demands on her time, it has been difficult for Kristi to practice as much as she needs in order to perform well in the 1994 Olympics in Lillehammer. She wants to compete but won't unless she feels she is ready. She expects so much of herself now, and others do, too.

"Kristi is her own toughest critic," her coach, Christy, said. "She may not show it on the outside, but inside is a woman burning with a desire to be the best."

"She's been more consistent than any female skater in many years," Kristin Matta of the U.S. Figure Skating Association said. "But what's most impressive about Kristi is that she's still the nicest girl you'd ever want to

Kristi speaks to reporters at a news conference.

meet. She didn't change a bit from the day she got to
Albertville to the day she left. And she hasn't changed
since. She seems so quiet but, really, she's just a happy
person."

Skating certainly has had a lot to do with that.
"Skating has brought out a side of Kristi that I didn't think
she had in her," her mother says. "She skates because she
loves to skate, and she has found a lot of happiness in it."

INDEX

ABOUT THE AUTHOR

Jeff Savage and a friend at the Louvre in Paris

Jeff Savage is a former sportswriter for the *San Diego Union-Tribune*. He has written biographies of Jim Abbott, Thurman Thomas, and Cal Ripken, Jr., as well as numerous magazine and newspaper articles. He is currently writing a series of fitness books for young people.

An avid sports fan, Jeff enjoys surfing, skiing, karate, and playing golf. When he isn't traveling, he lives in Rancho Bernardo, California.